Through Our Times

Through Our Times
Occasional Poems 1960-2017

Mark Busby

LITERARY PRESS
LAMAR UNIVERSITY

Copyright © 2017 Mark Busby
All Rights Reserved

ISBN: 978-1-942956-40-2
Library of Congress Control Number: 2017932053

Manufactured in the United States

Lamar University Literary Press
Beaumont, Texas

Acknowledgments

I'd like to thank my wife, Linda Busby, for being my best editor through our years and for her suggestions about this collection. I also acknowledge our son and daughter-in-law, Joshua Busby and Bethany Albertson, and their son, our grandson, Will Busby, for being Will and for always looking at the world with a sense of wonder.

I thank the editors of these journals for publishing some of the poems in this book:

> *English in Texas*
> *Studies in Poetry*
> *The Old Red Kimono*
> *Welter*
> *New Texas*

I have also drawn from parts of my fiction for the language and subject matter of some of the poems in this collection, including my novels *Cedar Crossing* and *Fort Benning Blues* and my short stories in *Texas Soundtrack, The Mayo Review*, and *Falling from Grace: A Literary Response to the Demise of Paradise*.

Other Books by Mark Busby

Novels
> *Cedar Crossing*
> *Fort Benning Blues*

Monographs
> *Lanford Wilson*
> *Larry McMurtry and the West: An Ambivalent Relationship*
> *Preston Jones*
> *Ralph Ellison*

to
Linda Whitehouse Busby
for all the years

Poetry from Lamar University Literary *Press*

Michael Baldwin, *Lone Star Heart*
Charles Behlen, *Failing Heaven*
Alan Berecka, *With Our Baggage*
David Bowles, *Flower, Song, Dance: Aztec and Mayan Poetry*
Jerry Bradley, *Crownfeathers and Effigies*
Jerry Bradley and Ulf Kirchdorfer (eds.) *The Great American Wise Ass Poetry Anthology*
Matthew Brennan, *One Life*
Paul Christensen, *The Jack of Diamonds is a Hard Card to Play*
Stan Crawford, *Resisting Gravity*
Chip Dameron, *Waiting for an Etcher*
William Virgil Davis, *The Bones Poems*
Jeffrey DeLotto, *Voices Writ in Sand*
Mimi Ferebee, *Wildfires and Atmospheric Memories*
Larry Griffin, *Cedar Plums*
Ken Hada, *Margaritas and Redfish*
Michelle Hartman, *Disenchanted and Disgruntled*
Michelle Hartman, *Irony and Irreverence*
Katherine Hoerth, *Goddess Wears Cowboy Boots*
Lynn Hoggard, *Motherland*
Michael Jennings, *Crossings, a Record of Travel*
Gretchen Johnson, *A Trip Through Downer, Minnesota*
Ulf Kirchdorfer, *Chewing Green Leaves*
Janet McCann, *The Crone at the Casino*
Jim McGarrah, *The Truth about Mangoes*
J. Pittman McGehee, *Extraordinary in the Ordinary*
Erin Murphy, *Ancilla*
Laurence Musgrove, *Local Bird*
Dave Oliphant, *The Pilgrimage, Selected Poems: 1962-2012*
Kornelijus Platelis, *Solitary Architectures*, tr. by Jonas Zdanys
Carol Coffee Reposa, *Underground Musicians*
Steven Schroeder, *The Moon, Not the Finger, Pointing*
Jan Seale, *The Parkinson Poems*
Carol Smallwood, *Water, Earth, Air, Fire, and Picket Fences*
Glen Sorestad *Hazards of Eden*
W.K. Stratton, *Ranchero Ford/ Dying in Red Dirt Country*
Wally Swist, *Invocation*
Lao Tzu, *daodejing* tr. by Breeden, Schroeder, and Swist
Jonas Zdanys (ed.), *Pushing the Envelope, Epistolary Poems*

Preface

Over the years, I've primarily been an academic writer and, more recently, a fiction writer. But throughout those years, I've written poetry, mainly poems inspired by a particular occasion or by a moment that caused me to recall some previous instance or idea. I published a few of them, but mainly I wrote them for myself. When I began writing fiction, I often drew on the language, subjects, and imagery of the stashed-away poems.

And then thinking about reading among friends at the Texas Association of Creative Writing Teachers in San Antonio in 2016, I decided to pull out that sheaf of poems and to alter my usual reading of fiction or scholarship and sign up to read some of my poems.

I was surprised and pleased by the positive reactions. Jerry Craven, director of the Lamar University Press, an old friend, a fine, dedicated writer, and innovative editor, suggested I go through my poems and let him look at the collection. This book is the result.

I've followed a loose chronological order, organizing the older poems and writing new ones to complete a sequence—youth, college, the civil rights movement, the JFK assassination, LBJ, Vietnam and the draft, graduate school, the writing process, the academic life from first job to full professor to research travels, and a topic I didn't realize was so often at the center of a poem—death.

    For this collection, I've recaptured the poems I had integrated into my novels and stories. I have also taken some scenes from my fiction and rewritten them for this collection. I hope the result captures my experiences of the latter part of the 20th and the beginning of the 21st century in a way that others will sense the large sweep of history presented through the small voice of a single figure listening to the jangle and hum of human suffering and joy.

CONTENTS

ix	Preface
15	Coleman Lantern
16	Spin the Bottle
18	The Cotton Mill
20	Doodle Bug
21	My Front Porch
23	Myrtle Cemetery
25	Dreaming Tom
27	The 16th Street Baptist Church Bombing, Birmingham, Alabama, September 15, 1963
29	November 22, 1963
31	The Clay/Liston Fight, February 25, 1964
33	LBJ I: Bring Lyndon Home, March 1968
35	To the Rain in Fort Polk, Louisiana, 1969
37	Toward Columbus, Georgia, October 1969
38	Low Crawl
40	Officer Candidate Training after My Lai, 1970
42	Rusty Calley, 1970
45	Notification Officer
47	Chicago Slow Pitch, Boulder, Colorado
49	On the Death of My Neighbor's Son
51	Mooning
52	Research
53	On the Market
55	These Are the Days When Words Come Back

56	On the Death of Spider Sabich
58	Politicos
59	In the Stardust Ballroom
60	Imeritus
61	Beaumont
62	Dallas
63	Assailing
64	Thalia, Texas, June 1979
65	The Sacred Hoop
67	Symbiosis
68	Moments of Unbeing
69	*On the Road*—Over a Half Century Gone
71	Grading
72	Christmas Tree
73	Kunta Kitty
75	Umpiring Little League
77	Heading West
79	Dreaming the Raft
81	Cottonmouth
83	Searching for the Past
84	Fire Ants
85	On the Island of Bachelors, Galápagos
88	When the Mail Comes
89	Getting Religion
90	*NINEELEVEN*
92	Where We're Bound
95	Dedication: A Wish for Will

96	Chasing Ernest I: Havana, June 2013
99	Chasing Ernest II: Paris, June 2014
101	Chasing Ernest III: Ketchum, Idaho, June 2015
104	LBJ II: Forgiveness, August 2015
106	From the Darkness of the Presidential Election, November 2016

Coleman Lantern

When I was a kid,
I thought the secret
of systematic success
was hidden in a Coleman lantern.
I didn't think that I
would ever be big enough
or smart enough to light
one of those fantastic filaments.

Big Miro, the Scoutmaster, was
always the one to light the lantern.
And I knew that it was some kind
of sacred ritual
into whose mystery
I would never be initiated.

And now, camped up over the Divide,
I see in my son's eyes
the glow of fascination
I used to have
when Big Miro performed
that mysterious rite
and lit the Coleman lantern.

Spin the Bottle

When I was growing up,
we often played spin the bottle
at parties in the community center
next door to the Optimist Club Swimming Pool.
That whizzing bottle was all the world then,
zipping round and round
past Sheila, Shirley, Connie, and Cecile,
as we dreamed it toward someone,
slowing it down or urging it forward
to land on her.
Then we'd walk her round the pool
hoping for a wondrous kiss,
We would move subtly up one side,
then down the other.
We would use the depth markers
to plot our way—
hold her hand at six feet,
arm around back at ten,
The kiss, if we were to do it,
had to come at thirteen,
or we were at the end of the round,
ready to begin again

and try to spin the world
until fantasies became flesh.

The Cotton Mill

Across Kaufman Street is the cotton mill
with its unctuous stench, polluting
probably, but back then we never knew it.
All we realized was that in the autumn
bales of cotton would appear,
stacked in rows like regiments
of raw recruits.

Then we would climb on them,
hide among them, charge through them
screaming "Rat-tat-tat!" and "Baroom!"
in that maze of cotton bales
until
the bales disappeared slowly,
soundlessly
moved into the cotton mill
row by row
where they were made
into the shirts and pants,
the fatigues and dungarees
that were worn away by others
—and later,

by
some
of
us.

Doodle Bug

As a boy, I'd visit my grandfather
and follow him out to the garage,
an old wooden structure
behind the house
in a perpetual state of decay and decline.
Out beside the garage
lived a hearty colony of doodle bugs—
little insects some called antlions or toritos.

They made inverted cones in the dirt
and when you moved the dirt,
you could see them
urgently seeking stable shelter
in the fine-grained soil
after their quiet homes
had been destroyed.

If you picked up a handful of dirt
and let it sift through your fingers,
you found an insect
that walked backward,
as if it were moving with its eyes
on the
past.

My Front Porch

When I go home again,
I know the front porch
will be as it always has been.

That porch is timeless.
A few more chips
in that porch-gray paint,
another warped board
arching up out of the flatness,
more vines twining up the screen,
but it will be as it has been
for the twenty years
I've lived or returned there.

When I sit in one of the rocking chairs there,
it's as if I've slipped through a time warp.
And those clasping vines over the porch
create an otherworldly, abiding dome.

I sit inside and I'm a flat-topped kid
wondering if my whiskers will ever grow.
I'm a skin-haired trainee on leave
and worrying about the war.

I'm a new father
marveling over our new son.
I'm a new graduate student
wondering about my next paper.
I'm a new teacher planning my next class.

On top of a water tower down the road
is a rotating light flashing in the night
and reminding me of a character
in a novel I once read,
a woman, who, like my mother
captured the web of darkness
in between the light,
commanding,
"Time stand still—here!"

And on that front porch,
it has.

Myrtle Cemetery

Here in autumnal silence
flesh become words

In Loving Memory

to wind into sounds
the sense of humanity gone.

At Rest
Asleep in Jesus
Gone but not Forgotten
Rest in Peace; Rest—in Peace; Rest, in Peace

So many take similar shapes,
struggling against a strangling silence.

Of a truth she was an example.
It's a little grave but O,
Have care, for world-wide hopes are Buried here;
how much of light, how much of joy,
Is buried with our darling boy.

So whisper lines of little Carl Tate.

Sing on sweet lines,
never end your song.

Dreaming Tom

A story glows in memory and dreams
about the night my father
bailed out of jail, Tom,
our black cook at the Corner Snack Bar,
for cutting somebody at a dice game.

In my dream, I see my father
go to the county jail to pay Tom's bail.
My father waits outside the jail
on a hot, sticky, and explosive,
moonlit night.
It looks like a city
instead of our small Texas town.
Up and down the streets
people look out of apartment windows,
and I think I see young zoot-suiters,
hepcats, men in overalls,
and pool-hall gamblers
watching from the darkness of the alleys.

The sheriff and deputy bring Tom out.
He's got a big black felt hat
with a white band and a long feather.

As he walks up to my father,
he swings the watch chain
and whistles some unknown tune and says,
"Hiya, daddy-o."
I think my father is going to hit him,
but father motions for him
to get into the car, our 1952 Studebaker.
The radio is blaring,
Elvis singing "Jailhouse Rock."
The Studebaker is low-slung,
Tom takes a home-rolled cigarette out of his pocket,
licks it, and strikes a match with his thumb.

As I wake, I try to recall more about Tom.
I wonder if the very quiet,
seemingly respectful man
who came to work every day
was actually a concealed, angry,
dangerous man,
one who would spit in the face of authority.
I also wonder if, in his heart of hearts,
he hated us, hated his job,
wanted to proclaim his true self
to the world directly,
that the real man was invisible.

The 16th Street Baptist Church Bombing, Birmingham, Alabama, September 15, 1963

I hear the old woman's voice:
"Last year 'bout September," she says,
"four little girls was killed
when a big load of dynamite
went off on a Sunday morning at this church.
One of those little girls who died,
Addie Mae, lived next door to my son and daughter.
And they was just tore up
by that little girl and the other three's deaths
just like they was their own chillen."

"So have they found who did it?" I ask.

"Hell, ever'body knowed who done it.
The Klan done it.
One of them bastards is called 'Dynamite Bob.'
But them po-lice
won't do nothin' to 'em.
One person was arrested,
his hand slapped and set free.
Four little innocent girls dead.

You asked me if things
was gettin' better,
and that's why I'm tellin' you.
Them little girls died.
Ever'body knowed the Klan done it.
The law won't do nothin'.
When black folks try to protest,
them Alabama cops
set the dogs on them,
turn these big ol' fire hoses on them."

Later, in 1977 one Klansman
who bombed the 16th Street Baptist Church,
Robert "Dynamite Bob" Chambliss,
was tried and sentenced to life in prison,
where he died.
Two of the other bombers,
Bobby Frank Cherry and Thomas Blanton,
were arrested in 2001,
charged with murder, and found guilty.
Cherry died in prison.
Blanton still lives, last I checked.
I hear the old woman's voice—
"Too little, too late.
Way
too
late."

November 22, 1963

After class that morning
I walked toward the college auditorium
on the campus square.
Just then someone in an old pickup
drove by and yelled:
"Kennedy's been shot in Dallas!"

A young student,
product of an uneducated family
in a small town south of Dallas,
I immediately had mixed feelings
—shocked by the news
that our President had been attacked,
but tempered by the virulent attitudes
all around me at home,
attitudes that made Dallas
an infamous city.

But I was looking at the world
through a narrow prism,
while around me,
the world flamed.
After the president was killed

near my hometown,
the world looked at us
as crazed hatemongers.
I told people who asked
where I was from
that it's a small town 190 miles north of Houston
instead of 20 miles south of Dallas,
where they grow
haters and assassins.

The Clay/Liston Fight, February 25, 1964

Excited by fight stories I heard from an old man
who lived across the street,
I wanted to listen to the radio broadcast
of the Cassius Clay/Sonny Liston
heavyweight bout.

Howard Cosell called the fight.
As it began, Liston strolled
across the ring right for Clay,
but Clay, with speedy footwork,
danced away from him
and landed good jabs
until round five,
when Clay protested
that he had something in his eyes,
maybe the cut goop treating Liston's brow.
Cosell sounded ominous,
since Clay couldn't see
to get out of Liston's way.

But Clay lasted the round,
stepped back inside Liston's sense of time,
and came back strong in the sixth.

Then Liston slank to his corner,
and when the bell sounded,
The Big Bear stayed on his stool.

Clay suddenly realized what happened,
leapt up, and danced around the ring,
yelling, "I am the Greatest in the world!"
"I am the King of the world!"
The fighting world was stunned.
Inside the next moment Clay announced
that he renounced his "slave name"
and proclaimed that he was now
Muhammad Ali.
And the rest
is
history.

LBJ I: Bring Lyndon Home, March 1968

I'm on a last trip around Texas,
a spring break road trip
from my East Texas college
to Marfa and Big Bend,
before I get the draft notice.

On the last leg to Austin to tell a friend goodbye,
billboards along I-35
proclaim "Bring Lyndon Home"
and make me laugh uncontrollably.
My friend tells me a local politician
running against LBJ's man
came up with this slogan.

We visit, listen to Shiva's Headband
at the Vulcan Gas Company,
and I pull out of Austin
on the last day of March 1968,
driving north, snaking slowly toward the interstate.

On the radio the station switches
to live coverage of an address
by President Johnson.

I half listen
because my anger at LBJ
clouds my head.

He talks about peace with honor,
standard stuff.
And then he says
with America's sons in the fields far away
he can't spend any time
on "personal partisan causes,"
and then:
"Accordingly, I shall not seek,
and I will not accept,
the nomination of my party
for another term as your President,"
withdrawing from the presidential campaign
and setting my mind on fire.

I would soon set out on my next big journey—
wherever it would lead me.
And then I pass another billboard
imploring,
"Bring
Lyndon
Home."

To the Rain in Fort Polk, Louisiana, 1969

It's almost like Gene Kelly out there
except these guys
are all young recruits
with fuzz on their faces,
and they're all wearing
those dirty olive drab
fatigues.

But they're singing and playing,
splashing and dancing,
shoving each other down
into the puddles,
throwing those dumb baseball caps
into the air
and watching them patter
into the pooling rain.

I'm sitting here under a pine tree
wondering if something mysterious
has come down with these showers
and infected
the April air.

At my feet the rain beats steadily,
flattening the flower sprouts
against the ground.

Toward Columbus, Georgia, October 1969

Out in the darkness
sounds are imperceptible,
flowing and merging, filling the void.
Gradually, the black fades
into a pale gray of jagged lines.

Sounds become more distinct.
Birds chirp and flutter in the trees.
A bright glow spreads across the sky
and then a bright arc.
Wind jostles the trees.

A whine forces its way into the din of the birds
and flutter of the trees, growing steadily,
filling the area, muting all other sounds,
deafening.
Above, the sun flames, an incandescent globe.
Then the jet lifts, blotting out the sun,
and I awake from uneasy dreams
to tighten my seatbelt
and rise
through
the
clouds.

Low Crawl

I always had more enthusiasm than ability as an
athlete—backup center and linebacker
for the Ennis Lions, shot putter in name only,
better handball and racquetball player,
passable softball and Chicago
slow pitch first baseman.

I'd like to think everyone has a sport
and may just happen to stumble upon it.
And that's what I did in U.S. Army OCS training.
A physical feat important only
to traditional military training,
evolving from WWI trench warfare
and archetypal assaults
against machine-gun nests in WWII,
low crawl had little application
to Vietnam jungle warfare
with little opportunity for quick, straight crawling.

To succeed on physical training tests,
you had to crawl forty yards in 21 seconds or less.
I consistently finished under 18,
while my fellow candidates, otherwise good athletes,

struggled.
I turned my fatigue shirt backwards
for more protection and less friction
and imagined the movement of an alligator.
But being close to the earth
with the soothing smell of grass
took me beyond the warlike intent
of the low crawl.

Officer Candidate Training after My Lai, 1970

We were off to a special class
in Infantry Hall at Fort Benning,
something about the Geneva Convention, hastily
arranged after the word broke
about the massacre at a little village called My Lai.
An Army lawyer captain from JAG,
who looked like Huntz Hall,
told a few jokes and then said,
"The first thing I want you to know
is that you can't kill prisoners."
My class erupted in laughter.
People slapped each other on the back,
clapped their hands together, and roared.
"No, no, men. I'm telling you the truth.
This isn't a laughing matter.
You must know the behavior
expected of American military fighting men
that reflects the expectations of a civilized world
and the Geneva Convention:
you cannot kill prisoners."
"Bullshit!" the class responded.
"Listen to me, men. This special class was instituted

in your training schedule
because of recent events abroad."
Members of the class stirred in their seats,
laughing aloud at the Captain.
Now he was not being funny;
he was hilarious.
For four months we'd heard stories
about torturing and killing prisoners,
so nobody found the Captain believable.
His comedic face and manner meant
he couldn't be taken seriously.
For us it was just another joke,
funnier than a sucking chest wound,
someone
up
front
muttered.

Rusty Calley, 1970

I passed the Judge Advocate General's office
and parked the nondescript olive drab Chevy
out front
near a short man in officer greens
sitting on a bench off to the side,
so short his feet didn't reach the ground.
His nametag confirmed he was Lt. Calley,
so I walked up, saluted, and presented myself
as his driver for the day.

Calley looked uncomfortable,
his eyes darting side to side.
"Ease up, soldier. Call me Rusty
and just take me to Miller's Discount Store
and then to get a beer at the Foxhole."

I tried to remember
what I'd read about him in the paper.
Calley had been in charge of an infantry platoon
company on a search and destroy mission
in a little Vietnamese village
called My Lai 4 a couple of years earlier in 1968.
They had rounded up a group

of old men, women, and children,
herded them into a ditch, and massacred them.
Just before Calley was to be discharged,
a chopper pilot who had landed at the village
while the civilians were being killed
broke the story to a *New York Times* reporter.
Calley was charged with murder.
His trial was being held at Fort Benning,
where Calley was under house arrest.

As we reached Victory Drive, Columbus' main road,
Calley pointed out a large discount store.
As we walked in, the many customers spoke to him,
and pledged their support.

An old woman pushing a grocery cart
addressed him:
"I just wanted to tell you, lieutenant,
that we love you here in Columbus.
We just think you're wonderful,
and it's terrible what they're doing to you."

Calley flashed a boyish smile,
bent slightly at the waist, and said,
"Why, thank you, ma'am, 'preciate your support."

"You shoulda killed 'em all. Wipe out the gooks," the grandmotherly lady replied.

Notification Officer

In the '40s movies,
it always came in a telegram,
(delivered by Mickey Rooney on a bike)—
"The Department of the Army regrets
to inform you…"

But when I was in,
we became those bits of paper.
In the movies the folks always knew
what to expect
when they saw
Western Union cycle up and set the kickstand.
When we arrived in our dress greens,
they knew too.

We were always briefed how to do it;
we were as fixed as those telegrams.
Polish your brass, spit shine your shoes,
get a haircut, shave close.
Go to the door, knock,
and when they come:
"I have some tragic news for you"
we were to say:

"I have
some tragic
news
for
you."

Chicago Slow Pitch, Boulder, Colorado

We're not really ball players,
more poets than athletes.
Jonathan on first built a domed house
up in the canyon
and found in the cross braces
a metaphor for the props
to hold up a world without order.
But Jon's hands are as sure
as a Venus flytrap.

And I suppose that's why
we are out here summer
after summer.
The world's
slowed down for a moment
as it arches, hangs,
and enters the strike zone.

That's what Arnie calls
the Existential Moment.
The order's there,
the outcome's clear.
And as you stand in center,

gloveless,
and watch that world come,
the path to alienation or acceptance
is as clear as the night sky
over the Rockies.

On the Death of My Neighbor's Son

Just before dawn, the hearse,
a silver-gray scarab crouching in the parking lot,
signals that my neighbor's suffering son
is dead.

I don't know him well,
but I've felt his anguish
as he waited silently
for this withering moment.

While the crickets out in the caliginous night
sing a canticle,
he comes to tell me,
quietly, inarticulately.
He stands, his body
softly wracked with
sobs of a sorrow
so deep that it
cuts through the heavy air
and leaves me
with an image of grief

I
shall
never
forget.

Mooning

Over the Rockies this morning
hangs a full moon like an orb
at the end of the world.

The wind flows
fluid and cool
toward the beckoning bright opening
while the liquid light streams
a mellow moving current
in my memory.
It draws me gently
into the mornings and nights
that I've looked up
at the full moon,
heard the owl's call
of mystery,
and thought of water, fecundity,
and intuition,
of transition from full to gone,
to that tiny fingernail moon
that always breathes
with promise.

Research

Today I watched
the man with the drill
working on the new addition
to the library.

Holding it before him,
he bore into the earth.
Round and round it whirred,
kicking up remnants of recent
and older times—
beer cans
barbed wire, bits of glass,
boulders, bones, rusty nails—
icons of ages uncovered by
the industry of human efficiency.

And on the front of the old section
of the library,
the motto reads,
"Who knows only his own
generation remains always
a child."

On the Market

There are so many of us.
We walk the carpeted hallways,
eyes at lapel level
looking for the wondrous names
of the wielders of power,
granters of jobs,
Zeuses of the industry
standing around godlike
paring their fingernails.
And down below
from Times Square to 47th St.
are the girls,
whispering, urging,
cajoling, offering,
just give me a chance.
I
I can do it for you—
uh-huh—
yeah.
Above are the fat ones,
the clammy ones,
the tenured ones,
puffing their hanging jowls

with professorial pomp,
mouthing the sounds uncommunicative.

And below are the girls,
watching,
whispering.

These Are the Days When Words Come Back

These are the days when words come back, flitting
first like finches on the horizon.
Soon they are robins, bright and lively, puffing and
pecking and then perching on the sill expectantly.

Then cardinals, they embody and move sprightly,
taking flight into the heavens
until they return,
descending darkly, ominously, deathly, like buzzards
or vultures
seeking carrion for comfort
and sustenance.

On the Death of Spider Sabich

He's dead, shot in the stomach in his expensive
house in Aspen.
Shot by his lover supposedly.

Like him, she's a slick cover face,
never alive, just smiling out from the racks
at King Soopers and Safeway.

I'm shocked but I feel little sadness.
Those magazine covers are lifeless,
unreal. They couldn't really bleed,
gag, choke, and die at 31.

They only live for the life
of the buck it takes to bring them home.
They only live long enough to become
dog-eared and flipped through.
They couldn't possibly hold a gun
and pull the trigger.

Their only humiliation is to lie
face up in the garbage
and suffer the indignity

of yesterday's coffee grounds,
this morning's egg shells
and bacon drippings.

Politicos

They are like old dogs,
these Texas politicians,
sporting deep scars,
old wounds
they lap and lick
lying on the porch
of the house.

Then their tongues
hang loose
beneath their flabby jowls.
They sniff the wind,
let loose an oily howl,
scratch, bite,
and then go round and round
looking for a soft spot
to lie on.

In the Stardust Ballroom

These are the crystal moments
suspended
in the mind
like round, cut-glass balls
hung from high ceilings.

Imeritus

They are the walking dead,
withered, pasty, eyes glazed
and pupil-less, like zombies
in a 1950s movie.

They walk into classes
and, like windup figures,
begin to lecture and quote.
They speak of love and life,
of morality and responsibility,
and then the veil of gray descends,
and they walk out
into their committee meetings,
their tenure and promotion votings,
their rendezvous and imbroglios,
mechanically, like those guards
at Auschwitz
who listened to Beethoven and Brahms
before they herded the masses
into
the
ovens.

Beaumont

West of here is Liberty,
but it is small
and insignificant.
Here the clouds
of refinery smoke,
like puffs from old cannon,
waft over the city in sniffs,
drifting down past the port
and the courthouse
where the motto reads:
"Liberty Must Be Regulated by Law."
T. Jefferson groans,
but Liberty is West of here,
small
and
insignificant.

Dallas

I look at Stemmons Expressway
and it looks back
with its mirrored buildings—
bronze and metallic glittering,
cold, flashy, austere,
ostentatious with Oldsmobiles
and Cadillac Sevilles.

They're supposed to reflect
the natural environment—
live oaks and Bois D'arcs.

But these multiplied, large looking-glasses
reflect
only
themselves.

Assailing

The moon rises brightly in Cleveland.
It is such a human act:
You leave the concert boisterously,
and I can see your brother's car,
probably a pink Buick with cheeky portholes, gliding
ahead.

Your wife assiduously sits on the accelerator.
As you bear down on the Buick,
you zip down your pants
until your bright bottom
waves its friendly greeting—
only to be illuminated
by the blushing lights
of the Highway Patrol.

You are not Ahab,
John the Baptist, or Hamlet—
more like Stubb, Flask, or Bottom,
pleading "no contest"
to the
exposure
charge.

Thalia, Texas, June 1979

No picture show or pool hall
quivers with any young life here now.
Most buildings have fallen into obscurity.
Thalia High School still stands,
but it too is closed, motionless.

Another brick structure has not yet crumbled.
On its face all I can make out
are the letters WOW.
That's probably what you said when you
gassed up your pickup
and escaped to
Wichita Falls, Denton, Houston,
and beyond.

The Sacred Hoop

With an unscheduled long layover at DFW
before my next flight to Atlanta,
I decide to go see the new Supercollider site.
In one of the magazines behind the seat,
I read about the new
Superconducting Supercollider.
From the map it's going right through the middle
of the little ranch that holds my first memories.

I rent a Pontiac and drive out
to see the old home place,
going through the middle of Waxahachie
with its coffee-table-book courthouse,
past the "Home of the Indians" sign,
fifteen miles from Ennis, my hometown.

The highway's four lane now, newly paved,
easy to see why this area
was selected for the Supercollider.
It's as flat as a disk,
as smooth as a piece of paper.
This Supercollider will circle fifty-three miles,
from Waxahachie arcing to Ennis and Midlothian

and Maypearl and back,
and it's all as level as a straight edge
with an underground tunnel
150 feet below ground.

On the flat, new highway, I roll
like Maxwell's demon, a self-generating dynamo
that produces energy in perpetuity.
Maybe we'll make voltage from hydrogen
and extract sunbeams from cucumbers.
They're going to use magnets to get quarks,
subatomic particles named by a scientist
with a sense of humor, traveling at the
speed of light and colliding with one another
to produce something like the Big Bang
and unlock the mysteries of the universe.
We'll know more about the
creation of the world
but will still wonder about
the significance of the sipapu
and
the meaning
of
life.

Symbiosis

My friend Jacob works
at the water treatment plant.
You get used to the smell, he says.
It's not too bad.

As a matter of fact, it's the most creative place
in town, says Jacob.
Seeds pass through the human body
into the sewer and at the water treatment plant
they bud and burst into fullness,
especially tomatoes.
Flushed marijuana seeds smuggled into
that fertile soil
sprout surreptitiously.

It's the most unified place around too,
says Jacob, everybody uses it.
Products of the whole town congregate there
where the smell is not so bad
and the tomatoes ripen abundantly.

Moments of Unbeing

A long time ago
up to the window of my self
I tossed a rope and then shinnied
into that fine and private place.

From there I saw being accrete,
become dimly incandescent with ordinariness,
as I watched the world outside.

But there have been times
when I've uncoiled that old rope
and like a spider's skein
let it down again
into that warm, dark, and fecund world
and learned to my surprise
that I am still alive.

On the Road—Over a Half Century Gone

Strains of language from the American night
carry back the sad, sweet memory
of Jack Kerouac.

But the beat doesn't go on, Dulouz,
speeding no more, the hammer not down.
How did you lose it?

For you Tokay wasn't
all right, its sweetness
coming up in a spasm
of bright hemoglobin
streaming into the toilet
you hugged that last time.

Hudson Motor's defunct
so's Cassady and Buffalo Bill.
Denver's pollution rises with
each bum searching for the truth
who thumbs in another clunker.
Larimer Street's a tourist trap.
Spit and the wind

blows it back
into
your
face.

Grading

Your organization lacks clarity,
is fuzzy and repetitious,
overlapping, and disunified.

Your thesis fails to be significant.
You have sentence fragments
and comma faults.

Your teeth aren't straight.
Your face is pitted.

You're sloppy and overweight.
Your clothes don't fit.

Your mind is mushy, and
you have too many spelling errors.

Christmas Tree

Yesterday, we put up our Christmas tree.
Its lights now sparkle in the tinsel
like tiny dazzling imaginations
scattered about a complex world.

There's a house, snow-covered,
hanging near the center on a straight,
strong branch. Nearby is a snowman
lit by a hard blue light.

Above is a Santa Claus, hanging so
he swings freely. Chickens, stars, angels
are suspended in beautiful symmetry.

No tygers burning bright appear here
either by day or night to shatter
the order of this world, but
the bulbs burn out
and the needles unfortunately
begin to brown and
fall to the carpet.

Kunta Kitty

My fat black cat disappeared
three weeks ago.
This morning a squawk and scratch
at my back door signaled his return.

Where have you traveled, black kitty?
Your flea collar twisted under your paw
like a leg iron has rubbed
a flaming slash on your now scrawny frame.

Were you captured by a slave trader
and sold down the river?
Did you bide your time
and then make a break for it?
Have you labored on a chain gang
in the cold December skies
with only your house coat for protection?

Whatever your adventures, now you're here,
no sunup to sundown in the tobacco fields,
just a bowl of cat chow, warm milk,
the squeals of rediscovery,

and the steady purrs
celebrating
home
again.

Umpiring Little League

The whole world is suspended in the moment
as I start the arm up, fist clenched.
Ten years ago I would've been a paunchy honky
parodying a black activist.
But today I am merely umpiring Little League,
and I call this 65-pound slugger out at second.

This is the all-American game, so he becomes
a snarling puma and leaps at me
in nine-year-old fury.
"He missed me! He missed me! You lousy ump!"
From the sideline I hear his father screech,
"You lousy ump! He missed him!
He missed him!"

My arm reaches its apex, and I pronounce the
sentence with pontificance: "Out!"
I turn my back to the slings and arrows of
antagonism and become Buddha-like
positioned behind first, arms crossed.

My son, the pitcher, goes into his windup
and shoots a ball toward home.

I watch its path with pleasing expectancy
only to hear the behind-the-plate ump,
supplied by the other team,
softly say, "Ball one."
And I snarl to myself,
"You lousy ump,
it was right in there!"

Heading West

Inside the letter from my mother
is a photograph of my stepfather
taken after he went home
from the hospital and lingered,
crippled and almost mute for several weeks.

He's sitting in the backyard under the pecan tree
in that rusty outdoor chair
where he used to sit to clean quail.
Now, though, things are different.
No robust grin now, the right side
of his face is slack, giving him a wry half-smile.
No healthy tan, his skin looks pale and wan.
I turn the picture over.
On the back Mother has written:
"Pop, two weeks after the stroke."

I turn it and something else
about the photograph bothers me: his hands.
I was always awed by Pop's hands
because they were huge, with a size 13 ring,
those hands constantly scratched and scabbed.

He'd complain, "Hell, with this onion skin
of mine, it's a wonder I got any blood left."

But what I remember most is his fingernails.
He could never get them clean.
He had worked for the railroad for forty years
before he retired to raise cattle,
and those nails carried rail grease
that probably went back to 1920.
In this picture, the grease is still there,
but the hands, like dying birds,
lie limply in his lap.

Above and in the distance
two cattle egrets circle.
They feed on insects around cattle,
I know, but they look like sea birds
three hundred miles
from
home.

Dreaming the Raft

The fog crept in soundlessly,
slipped around my room,
and snaked into the corners,
under the bed, into the closet,
into my bones, my mind, and my dreams.

Before sunrise, I heard the ducks
flying south.
I couldn't see them because of the heavy fog
that lifted from the river
and swirled into the sky in folds.
Their gentle sounds summoned me to follow.
I seemed to be floating down the river on a raft,
surrounded by that thick fog.

I had to shove away from the bank
pretty lively four or five times
to keep from knocking
into trees along the edge.

And then, I dreamed the fog cleared
and I was in the

open
river
again.

Cottonmouth

Fishing once in the Cedar Creek bottom,
I thrashed through the dense, thick briar and brush
—black hickory, ash, hog plum, sweet gum,
pin oak, dogwood.

Near the water, the East Texas lake smell
mixed with something else,
something vaguely familiar,
intensely unpleasant.
Then, a cottonmouth slithered
from under a rotting log,
its tongue flicking the air
under its foreboding, slit eyes.

The cottonmouth's musky smell
of rotting meat and rancid peanuts
caused me to remember
my father's story of a cottonmouth
mean enough to chase him up a tree.

Ducks quacked in warning
while blackbirds flew
in a perpendicular path

to a great blue heron.
A lake breeze cleared the air,
but I still felt an ancient chill to the bone.

Searching for the Past

I stand on a high cliff
above a vigorous river—
wide, deep, and muddy—
on a clear, windless afternoon
with a bright sun high overhead.

I cannot hear the roar of the river,
but I see a stark, black structure
against the clear sky.
Glowing darkly from within,
circular and black granite,
with no entry or windows.

I feel a deep mystery
and think inside this enclosed structure
is something I need to know.
I desperately want to enter
to find the guide, the person with the key,
but there is no one on this
high,
lonesome
precipice.

Fire Ants

Your mushroom-shaped mounds
are not very menacing.
Like tiny neutrons, you bounce off one another
in vigorous activity,
stirred up by the scuff
of my heel.

Then as a caterpillar drips off a leaf
into your midst, I see you fission
into a brown horde, and I know
why some treat you like invaders
from a foreign country.
Your mandibles are castanets,
your stingers cheap knives.

You roll her writhing body into the alley;
soon it's over and she's dead, a fuzzy lump.
Better to go quickly, I think, than
to wait twenty-five years for the cancerous
results of insecticide
or to spend a life treated like a carcinogen.

On the Island of Bachelors, Galápagos

> All that we can do is to keep steadily in mind that each organic being ... has to struggle for life, and to suffer great destruction. When we reflect on this struggle, we may console ourselves with the full belief, that the war of nature is not incessant, that no fear is felt, that death is generally prompt, and that the vigorous, the healthy, and the happy survive and multiply.
> —Charles Darwin

Our small yacht maneuvered
through the huge cruise ships
so we could visit the islands
after the masses have reembarked.
We would see the variety and serenity
of the Galápagoan diversity
without the hordes.

And so it was that we came upon the islands
with only the few of us
and with the remarkable variety
of the Enchanted Isles,
aka the Galápagos,
a variety of saddle that led the Spanish

to the name for the saddle-backed tortoises
that share the islands with the flamingoes,
pelicans, waved albatrosses,
red and blue footed boobies, iguanas,
the magnificent frigatebirds,
and the sea lions.

And it was along the cliffs of Santa Fe Island
that we first heard the distinctive moaning
that gave the place its designation as
the Island of Bachelors
and led us to learn of the story of the sad lot—
a scarred, bleeding, and moaning group of
unharemed sea lions,
the losers in the battle of the bulls
to be lord of the 20 or so cows of the harem.

The losers crawl off to the isolated
and lonely cliffs to lick their wounds
and regain their strength to try again
to be the one and only,
a glory that would not last long for the winner,
given that being the big boss bull required
lots of barking at interlopers to stay on top.

But soon enough, he too would lose the battle
and crawl off to moan with the others
and wait for the time
to regird the loins and
reenter the fight
for firm
but fleeting
dominance.

When the Mail Comes

I am a mature man,
sometimes even called stodgy,
I suppose,
but my hair has no bald spot
and my legs tremble as I
open this envelope
as if it were a dewy virgin.

And inside, is it—
yes, yes, yes!

Getting Religion

She lies back
in a brief bikini,
saying she's become
a born-again
Christian
and speaks breathlessly
of religion and redemption.

But all
I can think
is
Babtits.

NINEELEVEN

On Sunday *ninenine*, we passed easily
through the guards and into the exalted space
of the White House.
We were Texas literary types,
wearing boots and jeans,
invited by the first lady who'd started
the book festival in Texas
and had hosted a national one in DC
that weekend.
We slipped silently along the halls,
stopping at portraits of the flesh now forever
entrapped in oil on the walls,
some at Reagan, me at Jackie and LBJ.

Laura and George smiled and shook our hands
as we passed through the receiving line.
I told George it was too bad he had to get up early
to make small talk with us visitors.
He grinned, "No, you shouldn't ever
run for President if you mind smiling
and saying howdy to folks like you."
We snacked and laughed
and said our goodbyes

and headed to the Watergate, where
we Texas folks were put up,
filled with awe and irony.

The next day, *nineten*,
Linda and I got up early and headed
to Reagan National and winged back
without event.
So I was drowsy on *nineeleven*,
sipping morning coffee,
when the first plane hit the Twin Towers.

Katie Couric said the first word
was a small plane
had crashed into the building's side.

And it was about my third cup
when I looked up and saw the second plane
and knew that our world
was
irrevocably
changed.

Where We're Bound

> I Can't Help but Wonder Where I'm Bound
> — Tom Paxton

The once famous folk singer,
his long gray hair pulled back in a ponytail,
calls for the audience's attention
at this legendary South Texas music gathering.
He's to lead this Sunday morning congregation
of singer-songwriters
trying to get recognized on this small stage—
old and young, most with guitars,
a few with harmonicas,
one with a banjo, and another had a guitar
with mounted tambourine.

"This morning I'm lookin' back
seeing so many of you young folks out here,"
the host says.
"It started with Woody Guthrie for me,
well really Woody through Ramblin' Jack Elliott
and his album *Woody Guthrie's Blues*.
I played it over and over, especially *Ludlow Massacre* and *1913 Massacre*.

These songs got me started.
And then it was the Weavers and Pete Seeger
and Dylan and Joan Baez and
Peter, Paul, and Mary.
I did some hard traveling, all along the way."

He stops as a strong morning breeze
whips across the stage,
blowing the backdrop between his face
and the sun, the shadow
distorting his smile briefly.

"I been thinkin' backward,
rememberin' all the big events
of the last 40 years.
I met Phil Ochs at the
first Newport Folk Festival in 1959,
and I was there when Dylan first played in '63.
And I was there when Martin gave that
I have a dream speech in Washington in '63
and at Newport when Dylan went electric in '65.

"Me and Phil Ochs were in Chicago for the
'68 Democratic convention and almost got
arrested with the Yippies.
We did the freedom songs

for the voter registration drives,
did the freedom rides and lunch counter sit-ins
during the Civil Rights Movement,
and then I was there when the peace movement
protested the Vietnam War.

"I knew all the great singer-songwriters—
we all thought we was gonna change the world, that
music and thinkin' right
would bring social justice to bloom
like a field of sunflowers,
but all the flowers are picked and gone."

He stops talking and looks at the sky,
his face a dark cloud.
He stops again, rubs the goatee he's worn
for years, "The times they have a-changed."

"Do I regret any of it?"
He sweeps his hand
across the sun-streaked stage
and looks to the sky, smiling,
"I think I'd do it all again
the
same
damn
way."

Dedication: A Wish for Will

To my first grandson,
born August 11, 2011,
into a roiling world:

May you work
and play
in a world
with the best
of humankind's history
and with
only tales
of
the
worst.

Chasing Ernest I: Havana, June 2013

We're at the Ambos Mundos Hotel
in Old Havana,
where Hemingway lived off and on
for several years in the 1930s
and where he wrote *For Whom the Bell Tolls*.

The Ambos Mundos (Both Worlds) Hotel
has turned Room 511 into a museum,
and EH photos and memorabilia
fill the walls of the hotel.
We're here with a Texas literary group,
because the only way to get here
is with some legitimate reason.
You can't officially get here from the States,
so we came through Mexico.
It's only about 90 miles from Cancún
to the western edge of Cuba,
300 miles from Cancún to Havana,
and only the same 90 miles
from Cuba to the U.S.

But from the looks of the old cars in Havana,
the distance is 54 years.

When Fidel won in 1959,
he told Cubans if they had an American car,
they could keep it but could buy no new cars from
the U.S.
So they have kept them, nursed them,
jerry-rigged them again and again over the years,
replacing engines and drive trains
with parts from Soviet-era Ladas
and Moskvich cars.

We take a trip to Hemingway's home,
the Finca Vigia or the Lookout Ranch.
Reproductions of Hemingway's prized paintings
hang on the walls,
easy to view through the open doors.
And out back is Hemingway's boat, the Pilar,
named for the hard, old revolutionary wife
of Pablo in *For Whom the Bell Tolls*.
The Hemingways got out of Cuba,
but Fidel confiscated everything—
the manuscripts, the art, the library, the house,
and the boat.

Papa Hemingway was a man who lost everything,
eventually losing the ability to write one true
sentence, the strength to see the world

with clear eyes.
And so the last act was to place
that Boss shotgun against his forehead
and take leave of both worlds, all worlds.
He fulfilled part of his old dictum
that the world breaks everyone—
but not the second part
that afterward many are strong at
the
broken
places.

Chasing Ernest II: Paris, June 2014

We take the Luxembourg Gardens stop
and haul our luggage up the exit
and walk across the Gardens
where Hemingway supposedly captured pigeons
for dinner in those hungry days in Paris
in the 1920s.
June is beautiful in Paris, and we marvel
that we are here walking down
the Boulevard Saint Michel to our hotel.

We make the museums—the Louvre, the Orsay,
the Orangerie, the Rodin, the Pompidou.
And we make it to the Eiffel Tower
for a late night view of the city.
And on to the Arc de Triomphe
the next morning and then walk
along the Avenue des Champs-Élysées.

We see the graves of Oscar Wilde,
Gertrude Stein, and Jim Morrison
at the famous Pére Lachaise Cemetery.
And we stop at the Shakespeare and Company

Bookstore, no longer in the same location where EH
met James Joyce.

But it's still a vibrant place for literary events
and where we Texans hear a reading
from a big Texas novel, *The Son*,
by Philipp Meyer.

We get to Hemingway's bar, La Closerie des Lilas
on the Boulevard du Montparnasse,
and I sit at the bar next to a plaque
that identifies the seat as Ernest Hemingway's.
I order a Hemingway Daiquiri.
And when I get the check for the
equivalent of $24, I ask the bartender
the difference between the Hemingway
and the regular daiquiri.
He shrugs and says, "Le prix—the price."

Chasing Ernest III: Ketchum, Idaho, June 2015

We're searching for the Hemingway house
just off Warm Springs Road in Ketchum
up from the Big Wood River.

It's a private neighborhood
with a "Private Road, No Trespassing" sign
to warn off visitors like us.
But we nose our quiet Prius down the road
and stop briefly behind the house
where the great writer took his leave from life.

The Nature Conservancy owns the house.
On her death, Hemingway's fourth wife, Mary,
deeded it to them.
They tell us they're in the middle of plans
for the house,
but it's not open to the public.

We have more luck with the Hemingway
gravesites in the Ketchum Cemetery.
EH's grave is a low, flat granite monument

with "Ernest Miller Hemingway" and
birth and death dates covered with coins.

Nearby are Mary's grave, Hemingway's son
Jack's, and Jack's daughter, Margaux's.
She followed a sad family tradition,
committed suicide (a drug overdose) in 1996.
Her father, John/Jack/Bumby, side-stepped
the ritual and died following
heart surgery at age 77.

Out toward Sun Valley is the Hemingway
Memorial with a bust of Ernest and a plaque
with words EH wrote as a eulogy for a Ketchum
friend (and maybe for himself):
> Best of all he loved the fall,
> the leaves yellow on the cottonwoods,
> leaves floating on the trout streams,
> and above the hills
> > the high blue windless skies ...
> Now he will be a part of them forever.

I step up on the memorial base,
and Linda snaps a photo of me
with a silly smile and my arm
around the

great,
flawed
man's
bust.

LBJ II: Forgiveness, August 2015

I've moved into a new office in Flowers Hall
at Texas State—
Lyndon Johnson's alma mater.
My office overlooks a statue of a young LBJ,
with a photoshopped version
of the young politico—
his hair not greased and his outsized ears
reduced in size and angle.
I gaze out at the green,
mountain laurel-lined campus
and muse on LBJ.

As a 1A draft candidate back in the day,
I loathed LBJ, seeing him
as the ultimate embodiment of evil,
a small-minded man out of his league,
I thought,
with a Texas-sized ego keeping him
from following the right path of withdrawal
from the morass that was Vietnam.

I am a much older man now, older than LBJ
when he passed.

And I've read the stories of LBJ's steadfastness
in passing the Civil Rights Act,
and I've listened to the tapes
of his powerful persuasion
of uncommitted senators and congressmen,
cajoling and strong-arming them
to support the bill.

His vision was clouded about the war,
but his steely commitment
to the promise of a better future,
has softened my heart,
and as I look down on that image,
I murmur words of compassion,
mercy,
and
absolution.

From the Darkness of the Presidential Election, November 2016

Neither of my parents went beyond
the eighth grade, and I took my first part-time
job as a carhop at fourteen, then pumped gas,
was a drug store clerk and a paperboy,
and worked on a railroad road gang.

So I knew myself as working class
and held that a lower class boy like Huck Finn
could have a sound heart that would
discern truth from falsehood because
that sound heart would speak to him
and he, and I and others like us, I thought,
would know the road to travel,
even if we were poor and poorly educated.
The voice of common men and women en masse
would speak through the ballot box
and point to the way forward.

But my faith that the democratic voice
would speak the truth was shattered
like Ozymandias

in this election that treated facts like STDs
or Zika-carrying mosquitoes.

And now the Heart and the Mind take leave
of one another, the Mind going on vacation
in a faraway land, Antarctica perhaps,
while the Heart crawls out of the wreck,
and the Voice cries to the hazy sky,
calling out, "Save Obamacare!"
"Beware the hairy chest of the betrayer Putin!"
"What price bananas?"

May that Heart begin to heal,
may that Mind recover from the jolt,
and may the two trip along the spring jonquils
somewhere quiet and beautiful
and join that Voice to sing
of reason, beauty, joy, and
the return of the
legend
of
democracy.

www.ingramcontent.com/pod-product-compliance
Lightning Source LLC
Chambersburg PA
CBHW020945090426
42736CB00010B/1279